APEX PREDATORS
of the Amazon Rain Forest

Electric Eel

by Ellen Lawrence

Consultant:

Prof. Philip K. Stoddard
Department of Biological Sciences
Florida International University
Miami, Florida

BEARPORT
PUBLISHING

New York, New York

Credits

Cover, © Tom Stack/Alamy and © scubaluna/Shutterstock; 4, © underworld/Shutterstock; 5, © Mark Newman/Getty Images; 6, © Cosmographics; 7T, © Willem Kolvoort/Nature Picture Library; 7, © Dr. Morley Read/Shutterstock; 8, © Tom Stack/Alamy; 9, © Amazon-Images MBSI/Alamy; 10–11, © Billy Hustace/Getty Images; 11T, © Ruby Tuesday Books; 12, © Tom Stack/Alamy; 13, © Reinhard Dirscherl/FLPA; 14T, © Ljupco Smokovski/Shutterstock; 14B, © vagabond54/Shutterstock; 15, © Steven G. Johnson/Creative Commons; 16–17, © Mark Newman/Getty Images; 18, © Yourthstock/Dreamstime; 19, © Andrea Florence/Ardea; 20T, © Aleksandr Kurganov/Shutterstock; 20B, © DEA/G. SOSIO/Getty Images; 21, © Norbert Wu/Minden Pictures/FLPA; 22, © Ruby Tuesday Books; 23TL, © Ruby Tuesday Books; 23TC, © Billy Hustace/Getty Images; 23TR, © Robert Harding/Alamy; 23BL, © aastock/Shutterstock; 23BC, © Foto593/Shutterstock; 23BR, © Mark Newman/Getty Images.

Publisher: Kenn Goin
Editor: Jessica Rudolph
Creative Director: Spencer Brinker
Photo Researcher: Ruby Tuesday Books Ltd

Library of Congress Cataloging-in-Publication Data

Names: Lawrence, Ellen, 1967– , author.
Title: Electric eel / by Ellen Lawrence.
Description: New York, New York : Bearport Publishing, 2017. | Series: Apex predators of the Amazon rain forest | Includes bibliographical references and index. | Audience: Ages 5 to 8.
Identifiers: LCCN 2016049174 (print) | LCCN 2016050996 (ebook) | ISBN 9781684020362 (library) | ISBN 9781684020881 (ebook)
Subjects: LCSH: Electric eel—Juvenile literature.
Classification: LCC QL638.E34 L39 2017 (print) | LCC QL638.E34 (ebook) | DDC 597/.43—dc23
LC record available at https://lccn.loc.gov/2016049174

For more information, write to Bearport Publishing Company, Inc., 45 West 21st Street, Suite 3B, New York, New York 10010. Printed in the United States of America.

10 9 8 7 6 5 4 3 2 1

Contents

A Nighttime Hunt

In the Amazon River, a snakelike animal is on a nighttime hunt.

The electric eel has detected a group of piranha fish.

Suddenly, the eel releases a powerful shock of electricity into the water.

The stunned piranhas instantly freeze.

Then the hungry eel gulps down its **prey**, one by one.

piranhas

A Watery World

Electric eels live in the Amazon and Orinoco rivers in South America.

These long, wide rivers wind through the Amazon **rain forest**.

Many smaller streams branch off from the main rivers and flow through the jungle.

Electric eels make their homes in these watery places, too.

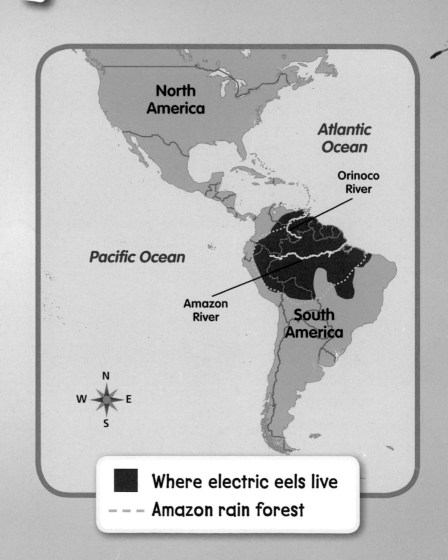

North America

Atlantic Ocean

Orinoco River

Pacific Ocean

Amazon River

South America

N
W   E
S

■ Where electric eels live
- - - Amazon rain forest

When rivers flood in the Amazon rain forest, the land gets covered with water. Then electric eels swim in the shallow, muddy floodwaters.

a river in the Amazon

Meet an Electric Eel

An electric eel's thick, powerful body can grow to be 8 feet (2.4 m) long.

It can weigh up to 44 pounds (20 kg).

An electric eel has a long fin on the underside of its body.

As it swims, this fin helps push the fish forward, backward, up, and down.

fin

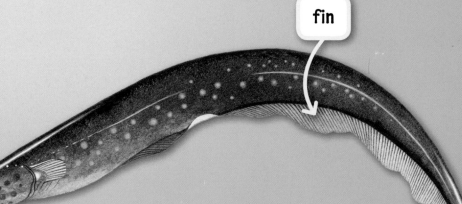

Unlike most fish, which breathe underwater, electric eels must breathe air. They have to swim to the water's surface to take a gulp of air about every ten minutes.

an electric eel breathing air

9

It's Electric

An eel uses its long body to make electricity.

Inside an eel are organs that contain thousands of special **cells**.

The cells are lined up like batteries inside a flashlight.

Similar to the way batteries power a flashlight, these cells produce electricity.

The electricity helps the eel attack its prey.

The eel doesn't just use electricity to attack prey. The animal also uses it to search for food. How do you think the eel does this?

cells that produce electricity

heart, lungs, and other organs

The organs that produce electricity are in the blue area.

An electric eel's heart, lungs, stomach, and other important organs are all located close to its head.

11

On the Hunt

An electric eel hunts underwater among plants and tree roots.

The eel has very poor eyesight, but it can still detect prey. How?

It produces a weak electrical field around its body.

The field can pick up the tiniest movements of a fish.

Then the eel knows which way to swim to hunt down its prey.

pits

An electric eel's body is covered with small pits, or holes. These pits allow the eel to feel the movements of its prey that are picked up by the electrical field.

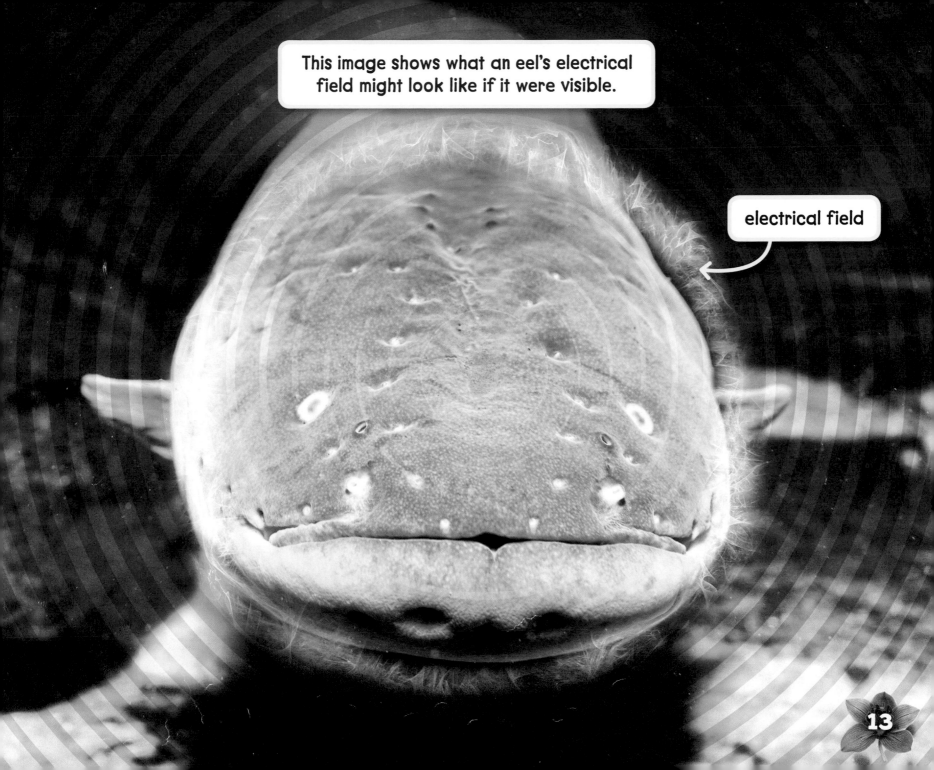

This image shows what an eel's electrical field might look like if it were visible.

electrical field

No Escape

To hide from a hungry electric eel, some fish stay completely still.

There is no escape, however, from the skillful **predator**.

The eel can send out a faint electrical charge into the water.

Then a fish gets a small electric shock, and its muscles twitch.

The movement gives away its hiding place, and the huge eel moves in for the kill!

discus fish

great egret

An electric eel mostly feeds on fish, but it will also eat other animals, such as frogs, rats, and birds.

an electric eel hunting

Zap!

Once an electric eel is close to a fish, it attacks.

It releases a shock of 500 **volts** of electricity.

The eel either releases the electricity into the water or touches its prey.

In less than a second, the fish is stunned or even killed.

Then the eel opens its mouth, sucks in its prey, and swallows it whole!

An electric eel's shock is four times more powerful than the electricity from a wall socket. It's even strong enough to stun an adult human!

catfish

In real life, the 500 volts of electricity is invisible.

17

Little Eels

Once every year, male and female electric eels meet up to **mate**.

The male eel makes a bubbly, frothy nest out of his spit.

Then the female lays up to 3,000 eggs in the nest.

The parent eels don't take care of the eggs, and many get eaten by fish and other predators.

When some of the tiny eels hatch, they gobble down the unhatched eggs!

a pair of electric eels

Baby eels are able to produce weak electric shocks. They hunt tiny fish, water insects, and other small animals.

a young eel swimming through a flooded forest

How do you think electric eels stay safe from predators that want to eat them?

Take That!

Young eels might be attacked by a large fish, caiman, or other predator.

The little eels try to fight back by giving attackers electric shocks.

Many young eels get eaten, though.

By the time an electric eel is an adult, however, it has no enemies.

The eel's electricity is too powerful.

If a predator attacks the big eel, the animal gets a nasty shock!

large arapaima fish

caiman

An adult electric eel is an apex, or top, predator in its Amazon home. This means no animals can kill and eat the eel.

The name "electric eel" describes the animal well. Can you think of another name for the eel that tells something about how it looks or lives?

21

Science Lab

Study an Electric Eel's Hunting Skills

An electric eel produces electricity for different purposes as it hunts.

Create a poster that shows an electric eel producing a weak electrical field to search for prey.

Then show the moment when the eel shocks its meal.

Add these labels to your drawings:

electric eel   prey   electrical field

electric shock

Present your poster to friends and family and explain an electric eel's amazing hunting skills!

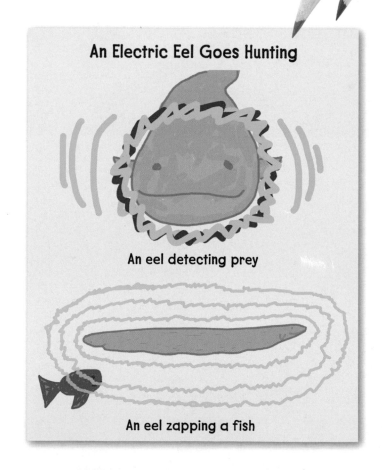

An Electric Eel Goes Hunting

An eel detecting prey

An eel zapping a fish

Science Words

cells (SELZ) very tiny parts of an animal or plant

mate (MAYT) to come together in order to have young

predator (PRED-uh-tur) an animal that hunts other animals for food

prey (PRAY) an animal that is hunted and eaten by another animal

rain forest (RAYN FORE-ist) a large area of land covered with trees and other plants where lots of rain falls

volts (VOHLTZ) units for measuring electrical strength

Index

Read More

Lunis, Natalie. *Electric Animals (Animals with Super Powers).* New York: Bearport (2011).

Roza, Greg. *Zap!: The Electric Eel and Other Electric Animals (Armed and Dangerous).* New York: PowerKids Press (2011).

Van Dyck, Sara. *Electric Eels (Early Bird Nature Books).* Minneapolis, MN: Lerner (2008).

Learn More Online

To learn more about electric eels, visit
www.bearportpublishing.com/ApexPredators

About the Author

Ellen Lawrence lives in the United Kingdom. Her favorite books to write are those about nature and animals. In fact, the first book Ellen bought for herself, when she was six years old, was the story of a gorilla named Patty Cake that was born in New York's Central Park Zoo.